The Amazing TRANSISTOR

Key to the Computer Age

Some Books by Ross R. Olney

Farm Giants
Construction Giants
Ocean-Going Giants
Imaging *(with Patricia J. Olney)*

The Amazing

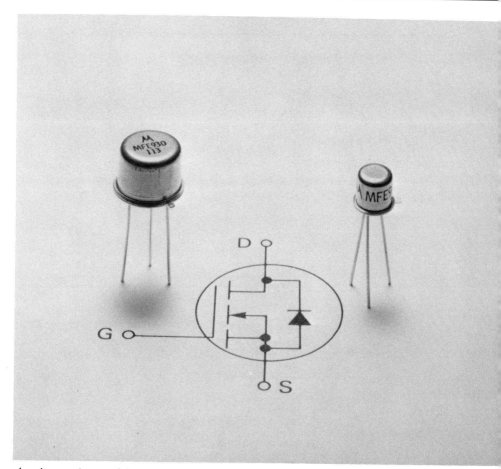

Amazing transistors and their electronic symbol. (Courtesy of Motorola Semiconductor Products, Inc.)

TRANSISTOR

Key to the Computer Age

by ROSS R. OLNEY
and ROSS D. OLNEY

Atheneum   *1986*   *New York*

Library of Congress Cataloging-in-Publication Data

Olney, Ross Robert
  The Amazing transistor.

  Includes index.
  *Summary: Explains how transistors work to form
integrated circuits that run computers and complex
communication systems and discusses the many uses of
transistors in the past, present, and future.*
  1. Transistors—Juvenile literature.
  [1. Transistors] I. Olney, Ross D. II. Title.
TK7871.9.046   1986   621.3815'28   85-27488
ISBN 0-689-31115-X

Published simultaneously in Canada by
Collier Macmillan Canada, Inc.
Type set by Linoprint Composition, New York City
Printed and bound by Maple-Vail, Binghampton, N.Y.
Diagrams by Harry Bates
Designed by Mary Ahern
First Edition

Ross D. Olney is a member of the Technical Staff,
Hughes Research Laboratories, Malibu, California

Contents

The Amazing TRANSISTOR

Key to the Computer Age

Guards control the gate between two fields that lets the crowd into the rock concert.

Chapter One
THE TRANSISTOR

Imagine a farm with two huge fields. Between the two fields is a fence with a heavy sliding gate. One field is empty except for a giant stage at the far end. On that stage will soon be a rock group getting ready to perform. All they need is an audience.

"Let's *go!*" comes a shout from the great crowd of people in the other field.

"Hurry up...*open the gate!*" someone shouts.

Nervous gate guards look back and forth at each other. The crowd is getting restless. They want to get into the field with the stage, to get a good position for the concert. Even though there are a number of them there, the guards are nervous. The crowd keeps getting much, much larger and surging forward, anxious to enter. Something has to *give*.

Then the word comes by radio. "Let them in, but *slowly* so that nobody gets hurt," is the order from the boss.

One guard steps up to the gate and pulls on it with all his might. It opens just a little, and a few people rush through and run toward the stage. Others are pushing behind them.

"Open up!" they are shouting. "Open *up!*"

The Amazing Transistor

Two more guards grab the gate and pull. It opens further and several dozen rock fans shove through. "Wider... *wider!*" people shout.

"Go ahead, *open* it," comes the order from the boss over the radio.

Several more of the gate guards jump forward and pull on the gate and it opens even more. Hundreds of people rush through and head for the stage. But then the word comes from the boss of the guards.

"That's *too many!*" he shouts. "Do you want to have a *riot?* Besides," he adds, "some of *you* are getting carried along with the crowd."

For every hundred people rushing through the gate, one of the guards is getting swept through.

So a few of the gate guards relax and the gate begins to close. Many of the rock concert fans who were trying to get through are blocked by the closing gate. Soon only a trickle of rock fans are still squeezing through the closing gate.

Finally, as all of the guards stop pulling on the gate, it closes. Nobody else can get through.

What has all this to do with a *transistor?*

Everything! If you can picture the fields and the crowds and the guards and the gate, you can see how a transistor works. For this *is* a transistor, or at least a simple picture of what an *amplifying transistor* does. It takes in a large, unformed current on one *pin,* forms this current (into a radio signal, for example) correctly with a much smaller current on another pin, and then passes the newly-formed signal out to the next part of the circuit on a third pin.

In the case of the other type of common transistor, the *field effect transistor* (FET), the guards would merely lower the entire fence between the two fields and everybody would run through at once. More about this later.

But first, here's a basic course on electricity. All matter, everything we know (including you and me) is made up of *atoms.* These are the "building blocks" of the universe. Every atom has one or more *electrons,* particles that carry an electric charge. In substances called *conductors,* which includes most metals, the atoms have one or more electrons that can flow freely from atom to atom. This flow is an *electric current.*

A transistor is an electrical valve, nothing more. It will either switch off or on, or it will make a current stronger. The more guards that pull on the gate to open it (though they are always much fewer in number than the total), the greater the number of people who can go from one field to another. But some of the guards will always be carried through in the rush.

The guards represent the tiny signal coming in to the "gate" of a standard transistor from outside, perhaps from a radio station. The people represent a much greater amount of electricity. The guards, the smaller signal, react on a gate inside the transistor. So a varying but much larger amount of electricity, the crowd of people, is allowed to pass from one point in the transistor to another. Coming out will be a controlled, formed signal exactly the same as that going into the gate, but much stronger. The transistor, with a larger, extra amount of electricity being supplied by your own power supply, has *amplified* the signal.

In the same way, the other type of transistor (called *FET* or *field-effect transistor)* can switch current off or on by allowing it to pass or not to pass. A current flowing between two points can be controlled by a voltage applied to a third point. The guards, the control voltage, merely open the fence entirely and the whole crowd rushes through.

Imagine a rubber tube with water flowing through it. You can squeeze off the water in the middle of the tube, or relax your grip and allow it to flow. The water is the current and your hand is the gate in this kind of transistor. You can close off the flow of water or allow it to flow on through, just as the electricity can flow or not flow depending upon whether the gate, the electrical signal, is open or shut.

In the standard three-layer amplifying transistor, some of the current from the gate is added to the flow (remember the gate guards getting carried through with the crowd?). In the FET transistor, there are only two layers. One is called a *channel* for

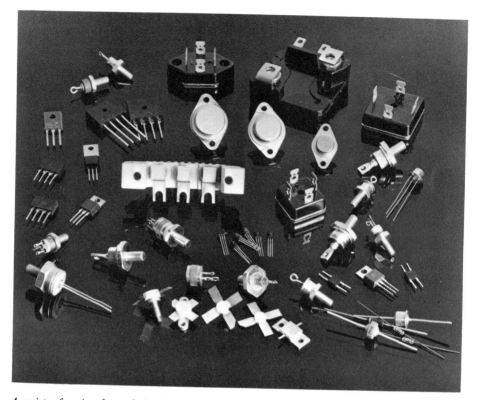

A variety of semiconductor devices (transistors) for a variety of jobs in electronics. (Courtesy of Motorola Semiconductor Products, Inc.)

the current to flow in (the rubber hose) and the other is called the *gate* (your hand) to start or stop the flow. It is a little more complex than this, but this is basically the way it works.

These are the two main transistors in your portable radio, your stereo at home, your wristwatch, and most other modern electronic devices.

The important thing is, these transistors electronically control and form the electricity they receive from your power supply. The light switch in your home probably works mechanically and does the same thing as an FET transistor. This works fine for a single simple light switch, when you want one bulb to be off or on. You could even run an entire portable radio mechanically if you had enough hands in the thousands of switches, or enough people who knew what they were doing.

But imagine how many people would be required to do the job. And just think how many hands you would need to mechanically operate the simplest calculator. Because the transistor works electronically, it can do these jobs instantly, and because it can be made smaller and smaller, thousands and thousands of them can be put into a tiny space. So, all circuits that use amplification and switching (and most do) can now be built efficiently into a very small space. On the other hand, what would it be like to carry around a one thousand pound portable radio!

There are many varieties of transistors. There are little ones so small that several hundred *thousand* can be built into a small chip of silicon. These are "computers on a chip." And there are large transistors to control huge amounts of power.

The simple digital wristwatch you might be wearing right now is a good example of small transistors. Not so long ago, your watch would have been impossible. Inside, electricity from a tiny battery is zooming about at the speed of light on marvelously complex courses. All of this wonderful action is going on silently and sight unseen. The result of all this switching of electric currents back and forth is the numbers on the face of the watch.

In huge radio and television transmitters there are very large transistors. These giants can get very hot, and they need a "heat sink" just to bleed off the heat that is developed by their action inside.

Television sets use transistors and so do radios, home appliances, automobiles, and more and more of the things we use every day. Transistors control the flow of electricity in these products. Most use transistors because they are smaller, simpler, cooler, faster, and cheaper, and because they use far less power to operate. Battery drain was always a problem with earlier portable radios, but now devices such as your transistorized portable can operate for months with tiny batteries. Portables of today can be small, even tiny, because transistors take less space and use far less power to operate.

Without transistors, we would not have pocket calculators or high speed computers. The computer that was used to write

Here are millions of transistors in their most prominent use, integrated circuits. Each device has many thousands of microscopic-sized transistors inside. (Courtesy of Motorola Semiconductor Products, Inc.)

this book, set the type, and print it used hundreds of thousands of transistors to route and control electricity to do the jobs.

Because they are small and lightweight, transistors have made space satellites possible. These lonely sentries in space, forever orbiting the earth, must be absolutely reliable. And they must require only the small amount of electricity that the sun can provide. They can pick up radio, television, telephone, or computer signals from one place on earth and send them to another place. There are "spy" satellites that can pick up the radio signals that are being sent on the ground, and aim them at transistorized receivers at another location on earth.

You've probably seen "dish" antennas in some neighborhoods, or on the roofs of some businesses. They are there to receive the signals from transistor-operated satellites in space, or from some other transistor-operated device on earth.

Without transistors, our lives would be quite different.

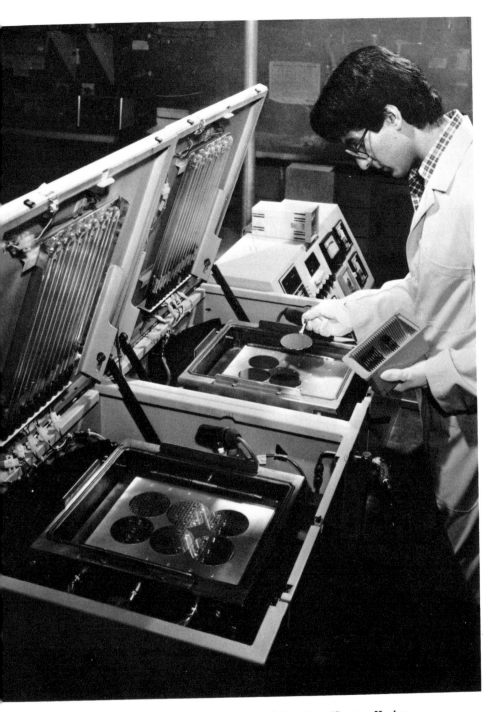

Making transistors is a precision job done by highly skilled workers. (Courtesy Hughes Research Laboratories)

Chapter Two
THE VACUUM TUBE

Before transistors, electronic equipment was controlled by vacuum tubes. The equipment still works in much the same way, but now the transistor does the switching and amplifying jobs better and cheaper. And in a much smaller space.

A *vacuum* is an area without air. Space, generally speaking, is a vacuum. Air (oxygen) is needed for something to burn. So a wire can be heated to red hot in a vacuum without burning in two. Inside a vacuum tube (in a partial vacuum, since nowhere in nature is there a "perfect" vacuum totally absent of air) is an *emitter* that gives off electrons when it gets hot. The emitter gets hot because it is next to the *filament* (cathode) in a vacuum tube, the wire that glows red hot when current is applied. Perhaps you have seen a vacuum tube glowing inside older equipment.

The action of a vacuum tube, with electrons flowing from the emitter to a *collector,* or *anode,* creates and strengthens (and even combines or separates) the flow of current. A signal goes in and is changed or modified inside, and comes out different, just as in a transistor.

From the 1920s to the 1950s, vacuum tubes were used in all

electronic equipment, and you may have seen them in older radios or TVs.

The outside of a vacuum tube is usually made of glass or glass-lined metal. Electricity will not pass through glass because it is a *non-conductor.*

Inside are specially designed wires and small metal plates that control the electricity fed into the tube. These are called *electrodes.* Each electrode is fastened by wires to a pin which is in the base of the tube so the tube can be plugged into the circuit. Electricity is provided from a power supply to certain pins in the base that are attached to the emitter and the collector and the filament (to heat the emitter and cause it to give off electrons). The electrons flowing between the emitter and collector become the same as the signal fed into the *grid* through another pin in the base, like the guards controlling the gate between the two fields.

The parts of a vacuum tube.

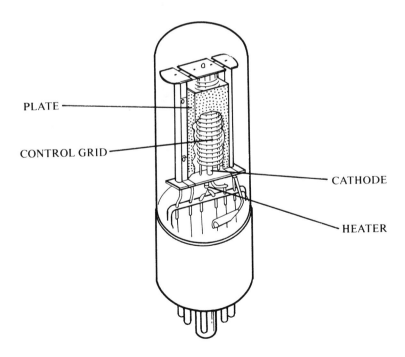

In the simple "triode-type" vacuum tube (three electrodes), the signal goes in through one pin. It is switched or amplified by the grid (the gate guards). Then it is collected by the collector as a much stronger signal and sent on in the circuit through another pin in the base of the tube.

The two main electrodes are the emitter and the collector (the two fields on the farm). The emitter usually has a negative charge and the collector has a positive charge. Electricity flows in and heats the filament causing the emitter to give off electrons. These electrons, going from negative to positive, flow to and are collected by the collector. To control the signal, the grid is added.

The grid is placed between the emitter and collector, just as the gate was located between the two large fields on the farm. The grid *controls* the flow of electrons between the emitter and the collector.

A strong negative charge on the grid prevents many of the electrons from getting to the collector, just as an almost closed gate prevented many of the rock fans from getting to the concert. If the negative charge on the grid in the incoming signal is reduced (opening the gate), many more electrons can get to the collector. The strength of the electronic signal being fed into the tube changes the charge on the grid.

There are also vacuum tubes with even more electrodes called cathode ray tubes. A TV picture tube is like this.

Such a tube has other parts that can bend and direct the flow of electrons. It is these electrons, being bent and aimed at certain points, that you are seeing on the face of a TV picture tube. The incoming signal from the TV station goes into the set where it is made stronger (by vacuum tubes or transistors) and then to the base of the picture tube. From there they go to the inside of the face of the tube and light up certain sections, and you see a picture just as it left the station.

Where did it all begin?

Chapter Three
A LITTLE HISTORY

"What am I ever going to do with *this?*" Tom Edison may have asked himself back in the early 1880s. The famous inventor had sealed an extra electrode into one of his electric lights. Of course he noticed that the electrons from the filament (the wire that glowed and gave off light) were attracted to the extra electrode (the collector) but he didn't know what to do about it. Edison had no idea of the amazing and far-reaching device he had invented.

Many inventions began this way. Edison had invented a vacuum tube, but he didn't even realize it. The flowing of electrons became known as the "Edison Effect," but nobody paid much attention because there was no use for it.

Then along came British scientist John Ambrose Fleming. In 1904 he experimented with the Edison Effect and found that he could detect "wireless" radio signals with Edison's invention. Fleming's tube became known as the "Fleming Valve," the first practical radio tube.

Lee De Forest advanced the tube in 1906 by creating the "Audion" (which could *strengthen* the signal), and Harold D. Arnold figured out a way to use the audion tube to make a signal even stronger in 1912. American Edwin H. Armstrong and German Walter Schottky added elements to the tube to make it even better. Then American Albert Hull advanced the vacuum tube even more. Along came Dutch engineer Benjamin D. H. Tellegen to continue to perfect the amazing tube. Finally Russian Vladimer K. Zworykin moved to America and invented the "Iconoscope," the first real TV camera tube, and the "Kinescope," the TV picture tube.

But then, along came the transistor, and vacuum tubes faded in importance. Eventually they will all be gone, relics of the past.

But for many, many years, vacuum tubes were in circuits to switch and amplify radio signals. They were heavy and hot and required large amounts of power to function, but they did the job well. Of course, they didn't last nearly as long as transistors do, but owners usually just looked in and tried to figure out which tube was no longer glowing. Then they changed that tube (at considerable expense, since they also cost much more than transistors). If they picked the right one, the equipment worked again.

There were even "tube testers" in many stores where vacuum tubes were sold. You could take out suspected tubes, bring them into the store, and "test" them. Sometimes this worked, sometimes it didn't.

All along, the trouble with vacuum tubes was that they were large, hot, and short-lived. Something better was needed.

Chapter Four
TRANSISTOR HISTORY

"Testing...testing...." You've heard it before. Somebody steps up to the "mike" and starts talking. His voice is normal, but it *booms* out from the speakers.

The whole point of a transistor is to control a larger amount of electricity with a smaller amount. Think of the transistors in a public address system. They take the weak voltage produced when you speak into the microphone and amplify it to a stronger voltage to operate the huge speakers. Then your voice will reach all the way across a room, an auditorium, or a park.

Current from the emitter flows to the collector and is controlled by the *base*. This is a name used in transistors but it means the same as *gate, grid,* or our old friends, the guards between the two fields on the farm.

Where did the transistor come from?

Sometimes good things come from a war. During World War II, new uses of the elements *silicon* and *germanium* were developed. These are known as *semiconductors,* compounds through which electricity can flow. It can't flow as well as through a *conductor* like copper, but it can flow better than through an *insulator* like glass or rubber.

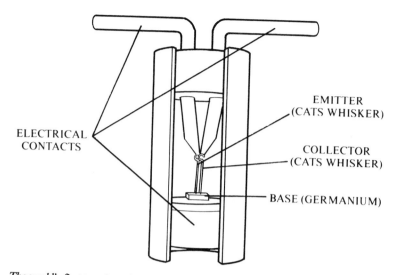

EMITTER
(CATS WHISKER)

COLLECTOR
(CATS WHISKER)

BASE (GERMANIUM)

ELECTRICAL
CONTACTS

The world's first transistor, invented by Walter Brattain, William Shockley, and John Bardeen.

Bell Laboratories decided to tackle the job of developing something better than the vacuum tube. Whatever it was would have to do the same jobs, but do them faster, cheaper, and more easily, be lighter in weight, and operate more coolly and more reliably. A tall order, but Bell scientists knew that they might find the answer in the semiconductor.

The task was assigned to three scientists, Walter Brattain, William Shockley, and John Bardeen.

After many experiments, the three came closer and closer to the truth. In November and December of 1947, the crucial experiment began.

"Brattain wrapped gold foil around a plastic knife edge and slit the foil with a razor blade to make two closely spaced lines of foil" said Bardeen in an article in *Science '84.* "This was pressed against a block of germanium that had an electrical connection at its base. A small positive voltage was applied to one line of foil (the emitter) and a large negative voltage to the other (the collector), both relative to the base contact.

"Holes (electric current) introduced into the germanium at the emitter flowed not to the base contact but to the collector and added to the collector current."

The three men had invented a brand new electrical device, made of gold foil wrapped around a plastic knife. It was primitive and could never be used in that form in equipment, but they had succeeded. Remember how the gate guards allowed more and more people to flow from one farm field to the other?

"Our device amplified by a factor of about fifty," said Bardeen.

The device was named by John Pierce, a Bell electrical engineer. At first he thought of "transresistor" and then he shortened the form to "transistor."

Finally came *planar integrated circuits* in which large numbers of transistors and their accompanying circuitry are built into a small chip cut from a thin wafer of silicon. Beginning in the 1960s, the number of circuit components that can be put on one chip has doubled almost every year. Today, the number has approached *one million* in one tiny unit.

Some chips and a woman's ring. There are more than a million transistors in this photo. (Reproduced by permission Zilog, Inc.)

Yet the cost of a chip has remained about the same. You can go to any electronics or hobby store and for only a few dollars buy one of the most marvelous devices ever known. Inside the tiny case will be thousands and thousands of transistors, all waiting to do whatever job they were designed to do.

Chapter Five
HOW CHIPS ARE MADE

Chips, which eventually will be made up of thousands of transistors, begin their life as sand and a huge road map. Let's follow one from beginning to end and into your wristwatch. They are a world away from the crude transistor of Bardeen, Brattain, and Schockley, even though these three men won the Nobel Prize in Physics in 1956 for their marvelous invention.

In fact, Bardeen said, "The revolution in electronics brought about by the transistor and related solid-state devices has moved far beyond the wildest dreams of any of us involved in the early days."

1. Silicon is the most common element in the Earth's crust, except for oxygen. It is plentiful and cheap. It is a hard, dark gray substance with the chemical symbol *Si*. It makes up the major portion of clay, granite, quartz, and sand. The sand on the beach is mostly silicon.

Silicon withstands heat well, melting at 1410 degrees Celsius, or more than 2500 degrees Fahrenheit. Jons J. Berzelius, a Swedish scientist, discovered it in 1823, though it was a long time before man began to use it to its best advantage.

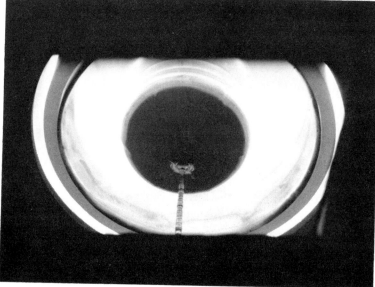

The silicon is melted down and a "seed" of single crystal silicon, mounted on a rod, is inserted into the molten mass and slowly rotated and withdrawn.

Left:
The first step in making transistors in integrated circuits is this shiny material called poly crystalline silicon.

After several hours, a nearly two-foot long ingot of single crystal silicon has been formed. This ingot is six inches in diameter. (Courtesy of Motorola Semiconductor Products, Inc.)

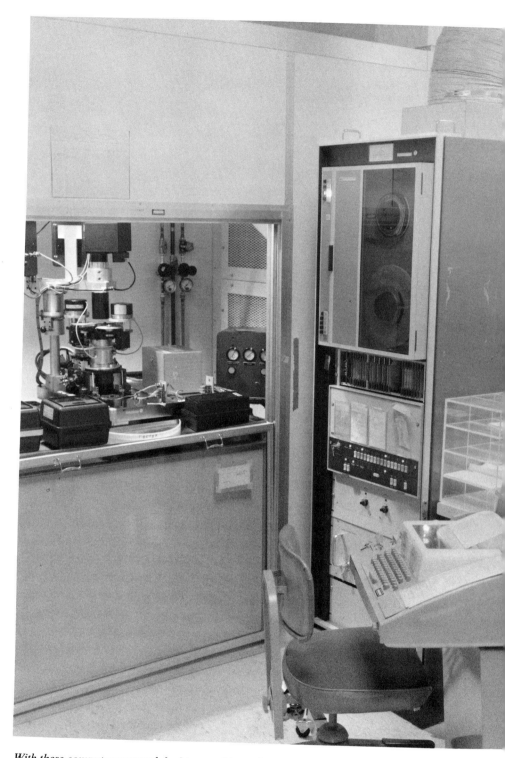

With these computer operated drafting machines, the complex artwork is prepared to make the patterns on the wafers. (Courtesy of Motorola Semiconductor Products, Inc.)

Silicon is the perfect semiconductor for transistors, and for chips made up of thousands of tiny transistors.

To get pure silicon, sand must be heated and melted. Crystals of pure silicon are formed and then cooked into the shape of logs. These "logs" are then sliced into very thin wafers and polished until they look like dark mirrors.

2. Meanwhile, engineers draw huge maps of the circuits, or paths, through which the electricity will flow. By making them very large, they can see exactly where they want the current to go. They can also make them *very* accurate from the first, since what they are drawing will eventually be reduced to a very tiny copy. Even the width of each line is important. Some are slightly wider than others, since the wide ones will eventually carry a little more electricity.

These large maps are called *photomasks*. They can be drawn by hand, or a computer will do it with the right instructions from computer operators.

These electrical road maps are then reduced to tiny, but perfect, imitations, by a form of photography. Some of them are so small you need a microscope to see them, but they are perfect copies of the large original.

The workers doing this wear clothing that covers them completely, so no dust or hair can get into their work. They work in "clean rooms" which are dust free. The rooms are many times cleaner than the most sanitary hospital operating room. Human hands never touch the wafers, for even a single microscopic speck of dust could cause the circuit not to work. In fact, if a worker touched these tiny items with the cleanest hands possible, there would be a mountain of grease on it when seen through a microscope.

3. With acid, the road map is then "etched" onto the wafer in many tiny copies, row upon row. But still there is no road, or circuit, for the electricity to flow in any of the little designs. So engineers create "wires" by covering the etched pathways with a thin metal coat, which allows each to carry the correct amount of current along the correct path.

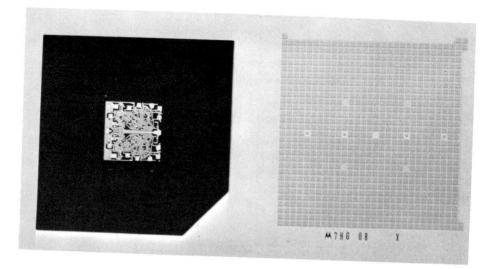

Above: One of the repeated patterns on the chip (right) is shown under a microscope (left).

Below: In a room many times cleaner than the most sanitary hospital surgery, these workers etch away, with acid, the unwanted portion of the wafer to leave the desired pattern.

Above right: After a layer of silicon dioxide is grown on the surface, the wafer is coated with a photosensitive material. A series of circuit patterns is then "printed" in this layer.

Below right: A critical step, this ion implantation equipment puts the right amount of specific elements into certain regions of the silicon to make transistors in the circuits. (Courtesy of Motorola Semiconductor Products, Inc.)

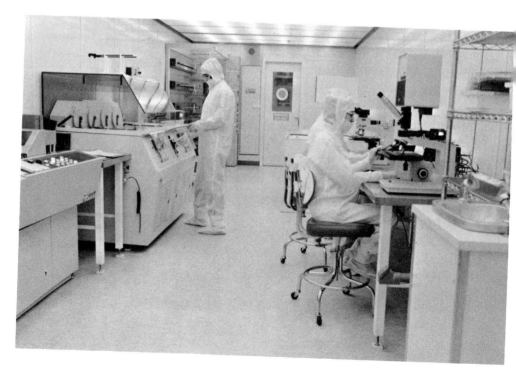

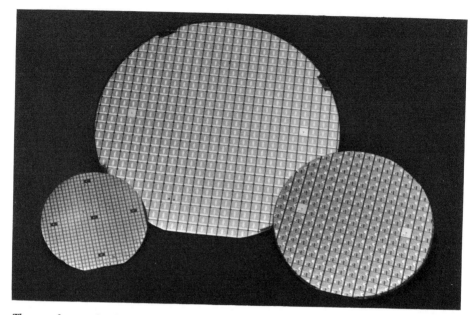

These wafers are finished, with the transistor forming elements in place. Shown are a two-inch (left), a five-inch, and a three-inch wafer. (Courtesy of Motorola Semiconductor Products, Inc.)

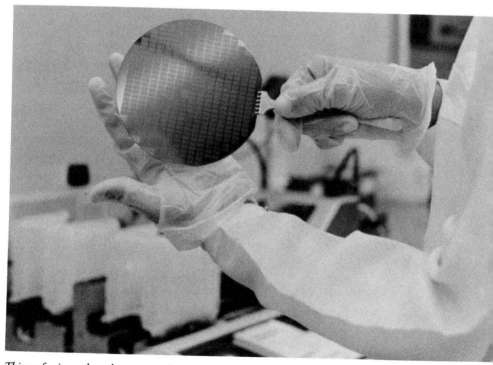

This wafer is ready to be separated into chips. No human hand ever touches them, for a mountain of grease would result (under a microscope, that is). (Courtesy of Motorola Semiconductor Products, Inc.)

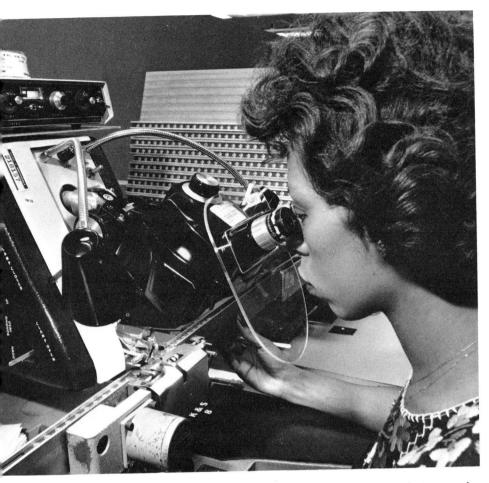

This "bonding operator," working with a microscope, is placing the chip into the integrated circuit. (Courtesy of Motorola Semiconductor Products, Inc.)

4. Next the wafers are baked in a gas oven furnace at more than 1000 degrees Farenheit. Tiny transistors, hundreds and even thousands of them, are thus created.

5. Then the electronic engineers may add another very thin layer on top of the first wafer and do the whole thing over again. They might do this several times, adding several layers to the wafer with each layer having various pathways for the current to flow and with tiny connections between each layer. The circuitry in each chip is usually too small to be seen by the human eye, but engineers know what is happening in the little devices.

Wires less than the size of a human hair are bonded to the chip and to points leading to the pins in the integrated circuit. (Courtesy of Motorola Semiconductor Products, Inc.)

6. Each wafer holds a number of chips, so the chips are cut apart. But not with a hacksaw or a kitchen knife. The people making the integrated circuits use a diamond cutter or laser (a tiny beam of light) to cut the wafer into separate chips. Of course, even then they are protected so that not a speck of dust is allowed onto the chip.

7. Working with a microscope (because the wires would be almost invisible), workers then wire the various layers of a chip to the contact points of the case.

8. Finally, each chip is sealed into a case. The case is usually made of plastic or ceramic (baked clay) because these substances are non-conductors and won't allow current to stray out of the tiny, delicate device. Gold wires finer than the finest human hair are attached from certain points in the chip to pins in the case so the IC (integrated circuit) can be plugged into a larger circuit. Gold is a very good conductor of electricity.

When the chip is plugged into your wristwatch, it is the same as wiring thousands of transistors into the circuit. But it is only one little device many times smaller than your fingernail doing the work.

Here is a microscope photograph showing the wires that connect the chip to the case in the integrated circuit. (Courtesy of Motorola Semiconductor Products, Inc.)

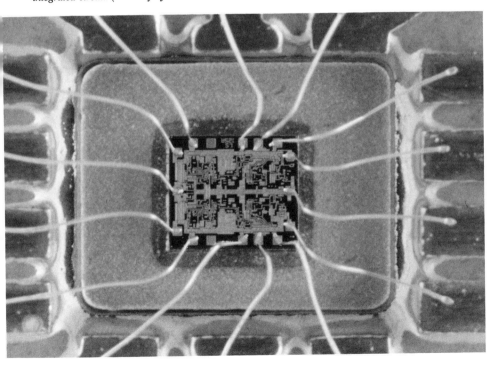

Chapter Six
DIFFERENT TYPES OF TRANSISTORS

Don't let the two classes of transistors confuse you. Some are called *NPN* transistors and others are called *PNP* transistors.

The people who make transistors bake certain impurities into the crystals of the semiconductor. These impurities control the way electricity flows in the circuits. Some impurities add extra electrons, called "free electrons," to the atoms in the crystals. Some do not supply quite enough electrons. They actually leave empty spaces called "holes" in the atoms of the crystals.

Of course, all of this is far too small to be seen, even with the finest microscope. Once again, the scientists know what is happening even if they can't see it.

A transistor is called an *n-type* if the crystals have extra electrons. If the crystals making up the transistor have holes in them, it will be called a *p-type*. Electricity flows one way in n-type transistors, and the other way in p-type transistors.

Imagine a row of pennies lined up side by side. Now, near one end, remove a penny. This leaves a "hole" in the line. Slide

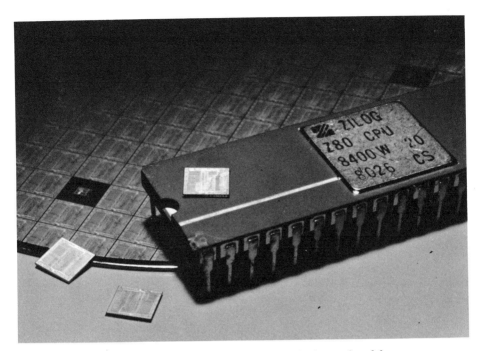

Note how much smaller the "chip" is, compared to the "wafer" (background) and the integrated circuit semiconductor device. (Reproduced by permission Zilog, Inc.)

the next penny over to fill the hole, then another over to fill the hole left by the one you moved. Do this all along the line, and you will get a better idea of electron flow. As the pennies move one way, the hole moves the other way.

There are three parts of a transistor, the base, the emitter and the collector. In some transistors, the base or middle is made of p-type material. Then the outside sections, the emitter and the collector, are made of n-type. This is an NPN transistor and in it the current flows one way.

Or the transistor might be just the opposite, with p-type material in the outer two sections and n-type in the base at the middle. This is a PNP transistor, and current flows in the opposite direction.

Whichever type of transistor is being used in a circuit, there are thousands of them in a chip, and often many chips in a piece

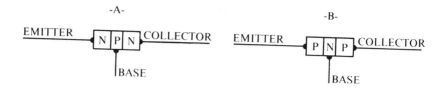

-A-   -B-

EMITTER — N | P | N — COLLECTOR   EMITTER — P | N | P — COLLECTOR

BASE   BASE

A — The NPN transistor.
B — The PNP transistor.

Diagrams showing NPN and PNP type transistors and how they are layered. (Courtesy of Motorola Semiconductor Products, Inc.)

A close look at a chip with its hundreds of thousands of transistors. (Courtesy of Motorola Semiconductor Products, Inc.)

of equipment. So a single piece of equipment, such as a computer, might have *millions* of transistors. Each tiny transistor has a job to do.

What if one of them, only *one*, fails?

Then that part of the equipment will fail. What if it is the part that eventually, through several circuits, makes the top of the numeral "8" in your watch? Then that part of the eight won't show up on the face of the watch. Each transistor, in spite of the thousands or millions of others, has a job to do and it must do it or the equipment won't work right.

Yet each transistor does a very simple job. In a computer, for example, each transistor must make one choice. It must either pass current or not pass current. It must say "yes" or "no." It must say "true" or "false." There are millions of true and false choices for the computer to make, but it makes them with such blinding speed that it seems to work quickly.

Let's take a look at how a computer works. And don't forget that a computer has many other parts besides its transistors. If *you* were a computer, your brain would be the *CPU* (the central processing unit). That is the chip in the computer that tells everything else what to do. But there is more than that to a computer. Suppose you want to complete a lesson in school.

The schoolbook you are carrying is the "software," which will tell you what to do. It may be a larger or a smaller book, but in the book is all the information you need to accomplish the job you want to do. Of course, you can only absorb so much information at one time, just like a computer. You have only so much "memory."

But that won't stop you, because you have arms and legs to get other books and to write down your notes.

A computer often has a "printer" to record information that has been processed in its CPU. You can read the book (the computer "boots" the information from disk to its CPU) and then write down your notes. If you need even more information, you can go to a telephone and call the library, just as one computer can call another through a "modem" attachment.

Software is like directions, or a recipe, to a computer.

Hardware is the machine that uses the directions to produce results.

Do computers, with their millions upon millions of transistors, ever make a mistake? Very rarely, if ever.

In almost every single case of a computer not doing what it is supposed to be doing, it *is* doing it. The computer, and the transistors inside, do exactly what they are told to do. Almost every case of a computer making a "mistake" can be traced to the one giving the orders. It does exactly what you tell it to do.

For example, if you set your digital watch to the wrong time, the watch, in spite of the thousands of perfect transistors inside, will go right ahead and tell you the wrong time every time you look at it. It doesn't know right time from wrong time. It only *keeps* time, and very accurately at that. The transistors inside are very good at counting the time. But they will start from wherever you tell them. You are like the software in this case, the watch is the hardware. The software tells the hardware what to do, and it does it.

Computers need instructions from the operator, and if the instructions are wrong, the computer will give you the wrong answers. A calculator, a small computer, is another example. You know that $2 + 2 = 4$, right? Let's say you want to prove it on a calculator. So you punch 2, then, by mistake, 3. The computer will give you 5 as the answer. It doesn't know that you made a mistake and hit 3 instead of another 2.

A computer needs orders from the boss to work. It is sitting there waiting to do wonderful things with letters and numbers, but until you tell it what to do, it is dumb. Computers get their instructions from software (information on disks or magnetic tapes from your tape recorder) and from you.

Each transistor knows exactly what to do but it will not do it, or will not do it right, if its instructions are wrong. You may be perfectly able to walk to a house around the block, but if somebody gives you the wrong directions, you won't get there. You'll get somewhere else. You have certain knowledge built in, just like a computer (you know how to walk and follow directions), but if the directions are wrong, you'll fail.

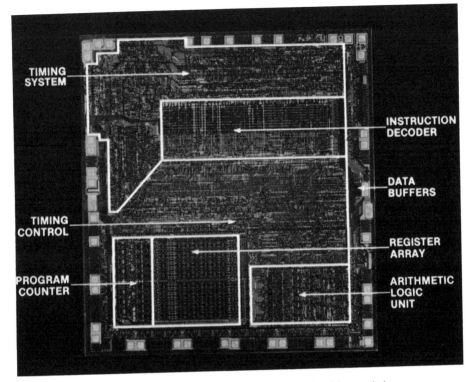

TIMING SYSTEM

INSTRUCTION DECODER

DATA BUFFERS

TIMING CONTROL

REGISTER ARRAY

PROGRAM COUNTER

ARITHMETIC LOGIC UNIT

The various parts of a chip do various jobs, as shown here. (Reproduced by permission Zilog, Inc.)

One new owner tried to write in a series of commands to order his computer to do a certain job. The instructions, according to the owner's manual, were this:

.y 1 110 90 5 60 0 0 0 1 0 0 0

So the new owner typed them onto the screen like this:

.y 1 110 90 5 60 0 0 0 1 0 0 0

And the computer refused to accept them. The owner went over them again and again, retyping them and asking the computer to work. But it refused. Not only that, it would refuse with an insulting "INVALID COMMAND" on the screen. And so the battle was on. Eventually, the new owner was sure the computer had malfunctioned. But he tried one more time after *carefully studying* the order he had given.

See if you can see what was wrong.

Here they are again.

The owner's manual—.y 1 110 90 5 60 0 0 0 1 0 0 0

The operator wrote— .y 1 110 90 5 60 0 0 0 1 0 0 0

It is a common mistake for a typist to make. Look at the 10th character in the instructions. Many typists use a lower-case L for the number one. That is what happened here. A simple and not very obvious mistake, but it was the difference between night and day to the transistors in the computer. The owner discovered the error and changed the final *l* to a *1*, and the computer instantly went into the correct program. Probably with a sigh of relief and a computer shrug of the shoulders at the carelessness of humans.

Here's another common typing mistake that we often don't see. It is the difference between a capital "O" and the number zero. But transistors in computers and other equipment see such a difference immediately. So modern electronic equipment, to help us and not the computer, puts a slash through the zero. Like this: capital O, zero Ø. The equipment already knew what we typed. Now we know too.

Chapter Seven
HOW IT ALL WORKS

You are a transistor. You are happily living with thousands of other transistors inside a computer. You have one single duty to do, otherwise you can just wait and enjoy life with all your friends. They also have but one duty to perform, and they enjoy it.

Your duty is the same as theirs. When you are called upon, you must make one single "yes" or "no" decision. That is all. You don't really care what the problem is, or what the computer is doing. But when the software instructions tell you to act, you act, depending upon what your friends next to you have done.

So let's all go to the football field together and sit down in the grandstand. Thousands of us will be sitting there together. Each of us is a transistor in a giant computer.

The voice comes over the loudspeakers. "Our job is to determine the answer to the following problem. What is the sum of 2 and 2?"

Easy, huh? But you will probably be called upon, because your job is to pass on a single yes or no answer. You are just as important, in this case, as every other transistor.

Remember, a computer does everything the hard way. So

This is a bottom view of a very complex integrated circuit with 149 pins, called a "bed of nails" grid array. (Courtesy of Motorola Semiconductor Products, Inc.)

you wait. Sooner or later (but still at the speed of light) you will be called upon to make a decision. You must act when two of your friends in the seats directly above and below you act. They, too, can only make yes or no decisions.

Here's the secret. You must hear their choice before you can make your choice and pass it on to the person sitting next to you. If the friend (transistor) above you says "yes" and the one below you says "no," then you know that you must say "yes" to the person next to you. And your "yes" answer is used by that person to report to the next person in line.

If the person above you says "no" and the one below you says "yes" then you know that you must say "no" to the person next to you. In this simple illustration, if they both say "yes" or they both say "no" then you know you must say *nothing at all* to the person next to you. That, too, will mean something in this giant human computer.

That's how it all works. Simple and direct. Each time you get a combination of answers from your two friends, you pass on your answer to the next person. Thousands of individual transistors are doing the same thing, and a result is obtained.

Wouldn't that take a long time? Yes, but remember, you are all working at the speed of light (186,000 miles per *second*), so it doesn't take long at all.

It is a little more complicated than this, but basically, this is how you, a single transistor, would work in a computer. You can test this with a small calculator. You can actually see the time it takes, even at that great speed, for such a problem to get to you. Let's change the problem for this test.

Punch in a 2, then a +, then another 2. Now hit the = mark. Almost instantly the answer 4 will appear on the display.

Your calculator will probably also "raise a number to a power." This is simply multiplying a number by itself a certain number of times. Most modern calculators will do this, even the inexpensive ones. So 2 to the second power is 4, or just 2×2. To the third power, 2 would be 8, or 2×4, and 2 to the fourth power would be 16, or 2×8. Let's do a more complex problem, one that will require the calculator to search for the answer. Ask it to find 2 to the tenth power by punching 2, then the right "power" button, then 10.

The answer is 1024, and on most calculators you will note a slightly longer time for the answer to appear. Not much, but a little.

Even though both problems are easy for us, the computer has done them the hard way. It has searched through many possibilities before reaching an answer. And though both problems are done at the speed of light, one will take ever-so-slightly longer to do.

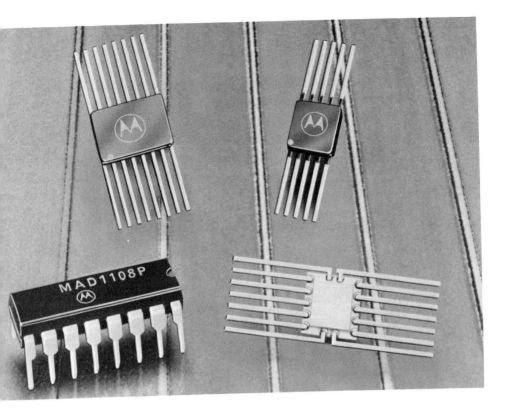

Different types of semiconductor devices (integrated circuits with many transistors).
(Courtesy of Motorola Semiconductor Products, Inc.)

Chapter Eight
TRANSISTORS
IN OUR LIVES

The truth is, without transistors our lives would change completely. Not just with larger portable radios, but in many ways.

Doctors use transistors in their equipment to monitor our health, to diagnose our illnesses, and to run operating rooms. Many other pieces of medical equipment are operated by transistors, including x-rays, dialysis machines, and other life-saving devices.

Our lives are affected by computers, and all computers now use transistors. Banks use them, schools use them, and more and more homes have computers. Your stereo equipment uses them.

Automobiles use transistors in the "transistorized ignition" systems, as well as in fuel injection systems, brake systems, air conditioning systems, sound systems, light systems, and many other devices in the car.

Airplanes use them not only to fly, but to land. In fact, there are modern systems that will land the plane by itself, right on the end of the runway. All the pilot has to do is watch to see that the

Here's an integrated circuit opened, showing the chip wired inside. (Courtesy of Motorola Semiconductor Products, Inc.)

equipment is working properly. Transistors help do this, and transistors keep airliners from running into each other in the sky.

Transistors are used in ground equipment to launch space flights, and in space vehicles to keep all the systems operating. You already know they are used in satellites.

No radio or television station could broadcast without transistors, and you couldn't receive the signal without transistors.

The clock that wakes you is probably transistor-operated, and the food you eat is probably transistor-cooked. If transistors don't provide the heat, they probably provide the controls. The clothes you wear were manufactured using transistors, for they are used in cutting machines, sewing machines, and even in the order and processing machines that brought the clothing to your store.

The stock market runs on transistors. Brokers and customers know the prices of stock instantly because transistors work the equipment. Banks can tell you your balance instantly because of transistorized equipment. The stores where you get your dry cleaning, where you owe money, and where you buy your food, couldn't do the jobs nearly as well without transistors. Even the clerk at the supermarket uses transistorized equipment (either cash registers or "scanning machines") to figure out your bill. Many toys now use transistors.

War machines use transistors, too. Missiles use them to rocket from the ground, to fly, and to find their targets. Warships use them to navigate and to fight. Submarines use them for "eyes" underwater and to launch their weapons. Modern soldiers use them for fire control, to aim their guns. Radar and sonar use them.

Scientists use transistors in their equipment to make our lives better. They use transistors to test and perfect new inventions, and to make everyday things work more efficiently. The gas company, the water company, and the electric company use transistors to get their product to us, and to tell us how much we owe them. Oil companies use transistors to search for oil, to drill for it, to move it to the refinery, to change it to gasoline, and to get it to the service station. Then they use them to measure how much we use, and to tell us how much it will cost us.

There is hardly a place left in our lives, awake or asleep, where transistors do not play a big part.

You can see that if they all went away, life would be different.

But they won't. Even today, scientists are working on newer and smaller transistors that will do more and do it better. There are transistors now being built using a mask so thin that you *can't even see it.*

Yet they still work the same way. The transistor is just a little device to control the flow of electric current.

It's a marvelous little device, pretty simple and straightforward, but working together transistors can do amazing things.

Index